Gravida

for Frances —
with much affection
& gratitude for all
your support over the
years — love, Sue
4 May 1995

Gravida

SUE STANDING

F O U R   W A Y   B O O K S
Marshfield

PREVIOUSLY PUBLISHED BOOKS:

Amphibious Weather, Zephyr Press, 1981

Deception Pass, Alice James Books, 1984

Library of Congress Number 94 -71638

ISBN 1-884800-02-5

Cover Design by Peter Fahrni
Design by Acme Art, Inc.
Manufactured in the United States of America

This book is printed on acid-free paper.

Four Way Books is a division of Friends of
Writers, Inc., a Vermont-based not-for-profit
corporation.

ACKNOWLEDGMENTS

Some poems in this work were originally published in the following publications:

Agni: "The Elegy of Doubt," "Six Values of Neutral Gray," "Wittgenstein's Prayer," "Patrilineage," "Coeur d'Alene," "Yusuf Abdulla Jaffer & Co. (Perfumers)"

The American Voice: "Bagatelles," "Men"

Columbia Magazine: "The Home Counties Posing as the Universe"

The Connecticut Poetry Review: "Letter to Hugo from Seattle"

Feminist Press Birthday Book: "The Anniversaries"

Graham House Review: "Windfall," "How to Ballroom Dance"

Harvard Magazine: "Because We Have Language"

Harvard Review: "Lamu"

The Iowa Review: "Translations from Colonial Swahili," "St. Francis in Ecstasy (Bellini)"

New Delta Review: "Jack Dracula"

Northeast Journal: "Foreshadow," "Plain Song"

Partisan Review: "Waterlilies in the Muddy River"

Pinchpenny Review: "My Sister Swimming Side by Side"

Ploughshares: "How to Be Angry"

The Poetry Miscellany: "How to Find a Name"

Poetry Northwest: "How to Use a Coma Kit," "Quarry"

Pulpsmith: "Desert Lands of Utah," "Holy Ghost," "Reena Baptima"

Quarterly West: "The Bones of the Plagiarist," "Palinode"

Radcliffe Quarterly: "Gravida," "Message" (under the title "The Latitudes of Light"), "Still Life (Fairfield Porter)"

Southern Review: "La Blanchisseuse"

Southwest Review: "Electra: The Escape Artist," "At the Gedi Ruins"

Texas Review: "How to Make a Planet"

My gratitude to the Blue Mountain Center, the Centrum Foundation, the MacDowell Colony, the Virginia Center for the Creative Arts, the Corporation of Yaddo and the National Endowment for the Arts for assistance and refuge during the writing of this book. Special thanks to the Duxbury group and to Lucie Brock-Broido, Peggy Hinkel, Donna Kerner, Allyssa McCabe, George Scialabba, and Jon Wilcox for their support throughout. Thanks also to Wheaton College and the Hewlett-Mellon Foundation for supporting a leave in the spring of 1992, which enabled me to complete many of these poems.

TABLE OF CONTENTS

I.

II.

III.

I
—

Arriving at each new city, the traveller
finds again a past of his that he did not
know he had: the foreignness of what you no
longer are or no longer possess lies in wait
for you in foreign, unpossessed places.

— Italo Calvino

BECAUSE WE
HAVE LANGUAGE

Dear Joe, Because we have language
I can tell you about the small flaw
in the pane of glass in my bathroom
which causes me to see the trees
outside that window as irregular
columns covered with spiders.

Because we have language I can tell you
about the chickadees and juncos
flourishing in the snow today.
I can tell you this:
here is my heart, my lexicon.
Here is the etymology of inspiration.

I can translate a Swahili proverb —
Mwenye *kovu usidhani kapoa*,
One with a scar, do not think him healed —
and you can give me these Russian proverbs:
The best fish is sausage. The best woman
is bird. The best water is wine.

But you say, "I am a jealous man of words —
I have one woman, one language."
I can only try to tell you about
the honeycomb inside a burning log,
the fire in which my words burn,
the black ashes drifting on the snow.

AT THE GEDI RUINS

Linger, do not go further, leave the gateway,
do not enter the ruins, you would feel sad;
if you call you will not be answered except by the echo,
human voices have ceased.

— Sayidi Abudallah Bin Ali Bin Nasir,
from the *Inkishafi*

After days of pseudo souvenirs — leather keychains
stamped "Jambo Kenya" and carvings of animals
boot-blacked to look like ebony — it's hard to find
what I want, though I know what I want: the real.

Not tropical as trope — dhows rigged out
as pirate ships or the gilded mildew
of tourist hotels — like a cultural comic strip:
but civilizations pieced together from potsherds.

At Gedi, the mandatory, government-supplied guide
knew nothing, worse than nothing — he got the few
facts wrong, made things up, supplied dates
for inhabitation off by a good thousand years.

But, then, later in libraries that might as well
have been in Alexandria, I found no explorers'
accounts even mentioned Gedi (some historians say
it might have been another name for Kilimani).

And no one can say what happened sometime during
the 17th century, except for scanty evidence —
all the storerooms were empty —
that the town was evacuated not stormed.

No one knows how many lived within the double walls,
the elaborate maze of palaces, storerooms, and mosques,
architecture reduced to abstraction,
a cross-section of a beehive or an anthill.

As to why they — apparently a seafaring people —
lived this far inland (Was Gedi a port that silted in?),
it can't be imagined from the moss-covered stones
of the wells

        arches

           keystones

cut from coral rag and red earth, even from fine-grained live coral,
and spanned by mangrove poles long since decayed.
Despite the labels, the skeletal rooms outlined
on the city plan refused to reveal their origins:

House of the Dhow   House of the Scissors
House of the Venetian Bead   House of the Cowries
House of the Porcelain Bowl   House of the Cistern
Mosque of the Three Aisles   Tomb of the Fluted Pillar

In the tin-roofed shed that serves as a museum
of dispossession, a few Ming bowls and celadon jars
put together from shards are strewn with iron knives,
a bronze eye pencil, and Venetian beads in battered cases.

Of the ancient graffiti scratched into the walls —
a lion, a bird, a dhow, a bed or a barber's chair —
only a few words remain to reclaim the lost city:
Gedi, "precious." *Linger, do not go further.*

L A M U

Speak of the bright white light, the sharp shadows,
        the carved plaster and wood, the zigzag stairs
        up the sides of houses like the houses you used
        to make out of salt clay in Sunday school

Speak of the sand dunes and coconut palms of Shela

Speak of the mangrove swamps ringing the archipelago

Speak of the southern cross in the sky at night

Speak of the patched sails of the dhows

Speak of the magic eyes on the hulls

Speak of the ladders leaning against coral-rag walls

Speak of the donkeys and chickens in the narrow lanes

Speak of the schoolchildren in parti-colored uniforms

Speak of the fragrant courtyards in which women live
        their secret lives

Speak of their hennaed hands, their rusty black veils

Speak of the intricate niches where the Koran is kept

Speak of the sound of Swahili like rustling palm fronds

Speak of the muezzin's five daily calls to prayer
        from the medieval minarets

Speak of the leathery feet of men so religious
       they won't even swallow their spit during Ramadan

Speak of the sweets put out to end the fast at dusk

Speak of the unphotographable graves

Speak of the ancient porcelain fragments you found
       near the Pwani Mosque

Speak of the corrugated tin roofs replacing
       the old *makuti* thatch

Speak of the dying coral reefs beyond the breakwater

Speak of the trade winds, the smell of jasmine

Speak of the voices lost on those winds

TRANSLATIONS FROM COLONIAL SWAHILI

A bad piece. A long arrow. Empty baskets.
Thick baobab trees. A hard bone. Heavy misfortunes.

She has beautiful buttons and a long chain.
The large islands have tall palm-oil trees.
The fierce drunkard has dry lips and a rotten head.

That arrow is broken. The basket has fallen down.
The baobab tree has fallen. The old person is dead.
The large bone is broken. The little child is dead.

The tall coconut tree has fallen. The cook is dead.
That drunkard has fallen down. He has built a house there.
This canoe is split. The child is lost.

Which baobab tree? Which chair? Which child?
What sort of bone is this? Which islands are those?
What sort of overseer is a blind person?

I have drawn a line. That old man dreamed.
The sweet potatoes have gone bad. You have tied yourself.
I have pained myself. Two thorns have entered the hand.

You will call the writer. The beautiful moon has gone down.
These months are good, those are bad. You were born.
I boasted yesterday, today I am sorry.

The mason built a secret room. Their spears are long.
The fisherman's heart is light. The man's voice is audible.
The children became blind. The broken water jars.

These bananas are redder and sweeter than yours.
He is weak today. It is true. A shadow which is not passing.

YUSUF ABDULLA JAFFER
& CO. (PERFUMERS)

for Donna Kerner

Down the narrow lanes near the old Mombasa port,
we walk past whiffs of rotting hemp and roasting coffee
while we imagine the southeasterly *kusi* carrying
its forgotten scents of frankincense and cloves.

Across from the Old Customs house near the dock —
where, for a few shillings, barefoot men balance
sacks of grain, pyrethrum, and mangrove poles
on their heads down the steep ramp to the quay —

and beneath the crumbling lattices of wooden balconies,
we discover a perfume shop, where women in *buibuis*
glide in and out of the women's mosque behind,
their prayers rising and falling like the tide.

The proprietor, a large man in dirty *kofia* and *kanzu*,
comes out to greet us. The one-room shop is lined
with glass-fronted cabinets covered by faded
technicolor prints of blond children and daisies.

We hope the man will offer us thick coffee
from a brass pot, and inedible silver-glazed sweets.
We hope he will open the mahogany cabinets
one by one, and dazzle us with crystal flacons.

Instead, he sits behind a battered desk in the corner
and pulls out a few small vials from a drawer.
But before he opens one, he begins to speak:
his father, grandfather, great-grandfather, all

were perfumers, an honorable business. Ingredients —
cassia, heliotrope, frangipani, ylang ylang —
came by *dhow* from India, Madagascar, and Zanzibar.
The words fall with difficulty from his thick tongue;

perhaps he's recovering from a stroke. He reddens
and his face bulges with the effort of speaking,
but he continues: *his* perfumes are pure essential oils —
not diluted, no alcohol to pollute Muslim women.

If you put this perfume on little little bit cotton wool
and place in ear — he squeezes up his face
and puts a finger in his ear to demonstrate —
will last for five six weeks. You bathe, you take out,

you put back in still fresh fresh after six weeks.
Like a Swahili Fuller brush man or vacuum salesman,
he tells us this several times before he begins,
finally, to open a vial of perfume.

By now, we've realized we can't rush the process —
Haraka haraka haina baraka, Hurry hurry makes no blessing,
the proverb says — and besides, despite the improbable
Disneyish photos on the cabinets and the man's plastic watch,

we've begun to feel as if we've entered another century,
far from the crowded bus terminals where we spent the morning
trying to find a way from Mombasa to the Tanzanian border,
seemingly impossible no matter how much *chai* we offer.

The perfumer first places a drop of orange blossom
on our wrists, then jasmine, then topaz, I think, though
I can't imagine perfume pressed from semi-precious stones.
Then there's myrhh, each scent darker, heavier than the last,

as if he were laying rich, embroidered brocades across our arms.
We can only afford one vial, and decide on orange blossom
like a Zanzibar breeze. Yusuf Abdulla Jaffer bows, and we
take our leave, *salama*, into the changing African air.

FROM THE FARAWAY NEARBY

1. The Cure

After the massage and the immersion
in the hot, sulphurous water,
I'm mummified in warm sheets and laid

on a narrow cot. White plaster patches
fixed like clouds on the green ceiling.
But nothing will cure me. Nothing

will make me buoyant and clairvoyant.
Rust spots floresce on the walls
like frescoes, as if I were in Pompeii

at the Villa of Mysteries, buried
under ash in the death pose drawn
by painters century after century.

2. The Procession into the Other World

She had no one to sing over her,
so she blackened her lids and went down
where her luminous limbs were strewn.

All along the river she saw the wrecked
cars tumbled beneath the bridges
like toys thrown over a playpen railing.

Through the tomb of the funeral couch
and the tomb of hunting and fishing
past the sarcophagus of the Amazons,

she went, the blue paint shimmering
on her skin like lapis lazuli, into the dark
sanguinary rites and dances for the dead.

3. The Museum of Last Resort

A mummified pigeon, dried-up pomegranate,
cracked leather, shards of faience,
hedgehog charms, a glass cucumber —

arrayed in the resurrection of a garden.
What I want — my limbs already stiffening
to bronze — is the echo of the musician,

her fingers curved to the lyre
when they find her in the Ur tomb.
Before returning to the begotten world,

I want to see that royal death chamber:
bowls of lapis, next to seventy-four bodies,
empty of narcotic drunk for Queen Shub-ad.

WAITING FOR WAR

for Jane Cooper

Through filtered windows
light enters the sarcophagus
Farther out, wars or the rumors of wars

I swim through the bony air
newsprint unfolds me
a disturbance of the sensorium

Radio waves of rhetoric
hum of American voices
a gavel *whereas whereas*

Make way for the *Sterbebucher*
more graveyards than vineyards
more boneyards than orchards

In the cold air off the arctic ice pack
the blue whales loom eating clouds of krill
plankton trapped against their flanks

In the Persian Gulf
sea turtles mistaken for mines
the vast sands navigated like sea lanes

Bright buoys beached on the dock
some shaped like canopic jars
some like torpedoes

The precision of surgical airstrikes
Remove their arms right and left
but leave the body intact

In Pompeii a perfectly-preserved skeleton
fleeing the eruption still clutches
a few coins in the bones of her hand

HOW TO SWIM AT YOUR OWN RISK

Be mole or raccoon,
sleek, blind, bullet-headed.
It's the simple that's dangerous,
the small objects with glamour:
the sheath of skin, integument of muscle,
under this skein of water.
You could get a blow so near the heart
or a blood blister in your palm.
You could spend a long time
looking for something better
than this small act of attention,
a long time making something better
than this small wake you leave
as you pull through your narrow lane.

WAKING IN THE SWAMP

Weighted under a net
of mosquitos, a double sky,

I could sink so easily
into the rotted logs,

into the loam of generations,
like the old blue sleigh

up to its runners
in moss and hot, soft needles.

Struggling to rise —
like a caterpillar hung

from a thread of silk —
I hear four squawks, then

a heron's heavy flight blurs
against the dark mass of trees.

HOW TO MAKE
A PLANET

Wouldn't a new planet solve your problems?
A small, solid, heavenly body. Take your timetables,
planispheres, untidy collection of maps,
and your devices to measure something-or-other.
Wait until the Great Rift Valley collides
with the Mariana Trench. Little by little,
dust will drift into a corner of your room.
A planetesimal, then a whole solar system,
will form in the *mare nostrum* of the double bed.
Once you were particulate, too,
little more than a thought. Now you want
to go where space is time, to see well enough
to resolve the double stars, following
the star tracks like geological strata.

MEASURING THE UNIVERSE WITH A BROKEN YARDSTICK

The five most frequently-used words
have been determined by computer, the way
so many things are now. At the time
I read about it, I wondered what people
fed in to make printouts spill like water
out of the terminals. Call it "x" —

not unnaturally — since the variable "x"
is the one most commonly used for words
or concepts unknown, even in watered-
down versions of theories that show the way
science works to those interested people
who ordinarily would not have time

to read about it, except in *Time*
magazine, which does provide good ex-
amples of the latest research by people
for whom "infall rate" and other words
like "collapsar" are the *Swann's Way*
of physics. They know that "heavy water"

is not the cloudy, murky water
left in the tub after the bedtime
of dirty children or on a freeway
after a rainstorm, and they know an x-
ray is worth more than a thousand words,
especially to those lucky people

who have been trained to read them, people
like you and me with eyes clear as water.
I once knew a girl who could not hear words
but had perfect pitch. She kept time
by feeling her pulse. Notes were her "x."
No one knew if she heard music the way

everybody else did. I suppose there's no way
to find out. I also knew some people
who claimed they could control their ex-
citement by thinking of underwater
refractions, but it's a waste of time.
I've digressed from the five words —

I'm sorry. Anyway (I'm pausing for a sip of water),
unless you're one of those people who has time
to fool around with x's and y's, forget the words.

PLAIN SONG

Sometimes we both catch a sleeping sickness
from the slow creak of porch swings, the heat
rising from the bodies of junked cars,

bulbs sprouting, forgotten, under the sink.
But today we wake in a triangle of light,
And the bay is the flank of a rainbow trout,

punctuated by the fisheye of an orange buoy.
In the rushy places, among signals of rain,
are swans pairing, cygnets brown as cattails.

NOVITIATE, CARNAC

How cool it was at Clermont,
with its nave of sunflowers
and choir of thrushes
whose sharp clear notes broke
over me like a waterfall of stained glass.

This abbey is too new:
bare, whitewashed walls and iron
grills that clang harshly,
echoing the overtones
when the Sisters sing compline.

When we pray, there is no sky,
and I am not allowed to walk
among the menhirs and dolmens
in the overgrown fields that lead
to Finistère — the end of earth.

In the sacred groves of oak,
diviners once cut mistletoe
with a golden knife and ferried
their dead to an island
in the Baie des Trépassés.

Before my heart, a standing stone,
splits under the weight of loss,
I will go back: in the ruined abbey,
I will lie in the flesh of breathing grass
and become as composed as the marble
faces of the broken saints.

ST. FRANCIS IN ECSTASY (BELLINI)

In the morning, the voices wake him.
A crack in the rock fixes the light.
He looks west with the egret and donkey.
A cluster of copper-green leaves
shakes above the fissure.
He forgets his sandals by the bed,
his open book on the table.

WITTGENSTEIN'S PRAYER

The world is everything that is the case.
Every sentence is in order as it is.
And there's no room for mystery in the place
the world is. Everything that is the case —
work, love, the truth — is evident at base,
a proposition like an answer to a quiz:
the world is everything. That is the case
every sentence is, in order, as it is.

II
—

We tolerate strangers because the things
we love cannot be touched by them.

— Bessie Head

HOLY GHOST

When I was a child I thought
the Holy Ghost never
got his chance: I wondered

why he didn't get a body
like the other two.
Was he a man or was he — ?

Why did he have to fluster
around inside my ribcage
& stop up my heart?

Why couldn't he just
perch on my shoulder
like a pet bird, instead

of worming his way into
my inner ear & pecking
at my thoughts? But sometimes

he was nice — telling me the answers
to pop quizzes. He flew
around the room looking

at the smart kids' pages,
then returned & guided
my pen to the right multiple

choice. "It's *axiomatic*,"
he'd whisper, or "*nirvana*,
not *Montana*!" Sometimes

he'd read books backwards to me
and tell me the plots of movies
before I'd even seen them.

He saved the best bits of gristle
& didn't make me eat
macaroni-and-cheese. At night

he tied his feathers to
my fingers & moved my hand
under the covers. My mother

was mad. I didn't know why.
He flew the coop when I
was eighteen & never came back.

LETTER FROM
THE ROSICRUCIANS

Dear Little Sister, When your eyes open
and you leave your calcified dense body,

the panorama of your whole past life
will be etched into your desire body.

(For more about vital, desire, and dense
bodies, send S.A.S.E. for pamphlet.)

Occult scientists and trained clairvoyants
have seen the soul can never be weighed

on physical scales though something unseen
leaves the body at the moment of death.

With a startling suddenness, the scales lift,
weighing the vital body, formed of four

ethers. From the time the cord snaps, the dense
body is quite dead, the fruitage of life

now draws to a close. One atom remains,
part of every dense body used by a

particular Ego. At death this Seed-
Atom rises to the brain, leaving the

body by way of the sutures between
parietal and occipital bones.

(For further information, simply write
for "Seed-Atom," $5.99, pre-paid.)

The chemical, light, and life ethers are
dynamically active. The fourth ether

has no thought or memory. There was a time
we set out concretions, as do mollusks.

Those who for the time being are in a
dense body of the feminine gender

have a positive vital body and
are more responsive to spirit impacts.

But until you are an initiate,
of course, you will never know whether this

is true. You will never know the intense
luminosity and vibrant power

of the candidate's brilliant auric light,
or the true compassion of advanced souls,

only the lesser mysteries of the
topical index in our latest guide,

available post-haste from headquarters.
Yours Spiritually, The Elder Brothers.

HOW TO FIND A NAME

In the beginning, my name was liana.
Then it was sparrow, then it was raining,
then time-before-light, and nuance.
They told me I was to-dance, but I forgot
footfall. I was dry as wallpaper, light
as dusting powder, but I had no name.
They called me come-quickly, called me dusk.
They called me full-moon and lifeboat,
they called me streetwalker.
They called me child-without-a-mother,
they called me not-to-be-taught.
In the end, it was whisper,
it was thunder, it was not-to-be-borne.

LA BLANCHISSEUSE
(TOULOUSE-LAUTREC)

The laundress pauses for a moment
to lean on the edge of her desire.
Her bleached hands grip the table
as she tilts her face to the window
full of a winter light that colors
her white blouse rolled to the elbows
and shines the copper in her hair.

The texts don't spell her name
the same way twice — Carmen Gaudier?
Carmen Gaudin? — this "thoughtful
working-class girl" who poses for you
against the tile roofs of Montmartre.
She has brought you a bunch of violets,
and you place one in your buttonhole.

After she leaves, you will go watch
Rayon d'Or and Pomme d'Amour dance
the quadrille like delirious orchids.
She will go home, take off her rough,
black stockings, soak her chilblained feet.
Slowly, dreamily, she will wash herself
and invent the life you paint tomorrow.

REENA BAPTIMA

I was born with tattoos, bright as new silk,
brought up by Christian missionaries
who tried to wash my sins away
with my tattoos. When that didn't work,
they named me Reena Baptima.

Freak shows are a thing of the past:
the three-eyed man died a few years ago,
Anastasia the monkey girl has retired,
and the alligator boy had an operation.
To me, the sideshow *is* the circus.

My body faded now to a net of lace,
intricate as tatting, except in water,
where I'm tropical, trailing colors
like a rainbow trout. The pictures glow
for a moment, then vanish as they dry.

I liked riding the circus train at night,
as we moved through towns too small to stop.
The train itself breathed like an animal.
I was never sad on the train — it seemed
always to carry me to a better future.

Sometimes I dream I'm back in the sideshow tent:
that moment before the curtain opened:
the hush before the gasp. Everyone wanted
to touch me, but I made love in the dark.
And when I die my bones will shine.

THE BONES OF
THE PLAGIARIST

are kept in a hand-shaped reliquary
made of plywood stained like pearwood
and studded with ruby-colored zircons.

What did the plagiarist plagiarize?
The history of tears. The lives
of the martyrs. The periodic table.

All on a ream of sphinx saxon manila.
The recent demise of the diva and her
castrato lover should not concern us here.

This plunderer cast his net wide;
his snares were artfully set.
His favorite game was snipe.

He rooked con brio, xeroxed with zest.
And when the end came, his last words
were certifiably not his own.

THE ELEGY OF DOUBT

Esther Williams, at 60, wonders
why her headdress of flowers
never wilted after repeated immersions.
Having another metaphysical lunch,
she dissects a word on her napkin,
makes anagrams of "natatorium":

I AT MAN TOUR, MOUNT ATRIA,
TO A MAIN RUT, AT NO ATRIUM.
A swim will make her life come right;

"Swimmer, on your mark," her favorite words.
She wonders what it would be like
to be a fish with a swim bladder,

what it would be like to swim forever
underwater and never have to reach
for the red emergency ladder.

She holds her breath and thinks she sees,
above the hanging gardens of Babylon,
a giant fingerprint smudging the sky.

H O W T O B E A N G R Y

Instructions for this hour: First, breathe
as shallowly as you can. Pretend you hear
the sound of a door slamming over and over,
its bright clang, then muffled reverberation.
Your heart beats more quickly until your hands
make involuntary fists that knock against each other
like the hearts of strangers. Second, pretend
you are a diamondback rattler. Narrow your eyes.
Be one long sinew of focused malice, your glance
a wedge of muscle pressed against your enemy.
Then, think of cold air whirring through cracks,
dinosaur eggs unhatched in Montana buttes,
the anteater's tongue, the bullet holes
in a target, the lies in your enemy's mouth.

ELECTRA:
THE ESCAPE ARTIST

Once I was the sorcerer's apprentice;
I wore a spangled dress and sequined hair,
and caught a bullet lightly as a kiss.

The sorcerer acted *in loco parentis*,
raising me under his false thumbs, his stare.
He wanted the perfect sorcerer's apprentice.

I started sawing men in half, against his wish,
and I made them vanish in the bright air,
the way I caught a bullet easy as a kiss.

I learned to juggle knives and never miss,
to escape from straitjackets at the fair,
after I ceased to be the sorcerer's apprentice.

I hung upside-down from burning ropes — the hiss
of fire pleased me more than his caress or care —
having learned to catch a bullet lightly as a kiss.

I tell my fans it takes a little practice,
a body supple as Houdini's, and a certain flair.
Once I was the sorcerer's apprentice
who caught a bullet lightly as a kiss.

M E N

after Ritsos

Men are very distant.
Their cars smell of goodbye.
They set the money on the table
so that we don't feel their absence.

Men are like packages
you don't want to open,
or books you can't allow
yourself to read.

They sleep in black yak-hair tents
and hunt blue sheep.
They stay in motor courts
and drink cheap whiskey.

Men live inside maps
and have eyes like gas flames.
It's amazing what they can burn
with one match.

JACK DRACULA

Nilla always razzes me about my "Live Free or Die"
tattoo. She says, "Live free, or die tattooed."
"Live by the pen and die by the sword," I snap back.

(She's a writer.) "Jack Dracula, the Marked Man,"
she calls me. But secretly she likes the fact
that under the tattoos, I look a bit like James Dean.

(We have the same initials and pompadour.) I think
he would have liked the eagle pecking at the skin
above my right nipple, the mock goggles and sideburns,

my ornamental mustache of stars, the spiderweb centered
around my left elbow. Tattoos are a kind of badge,
an initiation into the mysteries of flesh and mortality —

and even Nilla knows that. I've asked her to photograph
me lying on my side in the tall grass of late summer.
I look straight at her, stalking her, baiting her.

I want to be remembered. I want the two bats circling
my ribs — "Dracula" and "The Best" — to be legible.
I want her to think of my cold and incubate kisses.

HOW TO
BALLROOM DANCE

Sift through the satellite disks of records.
Choose only the heavy ones, the 78's.
Your dancing partner smells of rosewater
and burnt ironing. Angular shoulder blades.
The orchestra, your imagined orchestra,
is nowhere to be found. But near the bandstand:
a scent of gardenias, a faint metallic smell,
and a crackly feel to the air as if electricity
had just passed through it. Your partner
asks if you are wearing Evening in Paris.
You keep following the footprints, step-slide,
step-slide, until you dance over the edge
of the Starlite Roof, across the cut paper
silhouette of the fractionally full moon.

THE PHYSICIAN

There were so many like you —
healers-of-wounds, ones-who-will-not-die,

secure in your sepia-walled rooms
varnished like old library globes —

against the one for whom language
was a drug: nepenthe.

To counter my fear of breaking
into bits of bread of breath

of molecules of atoms too small
to be seen under your microscopes,

I wanted an old-fashioned diagnosis,
not spectrochromatography.

It was never for history
I gave you a blank slate.

Since I have neither rosary nor mantra,
I was seeking some kind of order —

classifying birds or barbarities,
anything to name again and again.

STILL LIFE
(FAIRFIELD PORTER)

Today, he wants to paint snow.
Beside him on the breakfast table
next to the jam and sugar is a book:
Opus Posthumous. "We live in the mind"

and "Poetry is the cure of the mind,"
it says. No one is the poet of snow,
if not Stevens. The painter opens the book,
then closes it. He looks at the table

where lemons and limes form a tableau.
The color of the cloth reminds
him of the bluewhite of new snow.
He gets out pastels and sketchbook.

He removes the fruit and the book,
but then the cloth on the table
loses its blue shadows. "... the mind
is all toward abstraction." The snow?

The snow he will keep in mind
while he paints the book on the table.

SIX VALUES OF
NEUTRAL GRAY

The sea, far off, with its rooms and strangers.
Where words recede under the muscle of tide.

In clear moments, I remember your studio
and you in the doorway. If I had not left,

would you have stayed and not turned back
to your blunt vocabulary of strokes,

your monochrome palette. The unmade bed,
a few hairpins arranged on the sheet.

Bight, slip, seawall. We were so quick
to learn each other's imperfections.

Six rooms, six paintings. The shadows grow
more opaque. Nothing that can't be painted out.

MESSAGE

First frost, and then the latitudes of light
contract. Outside my window a wash of leaves
spills over the bedrock like fish astride
last summer's waterfall. Up in the eaves,
a few oak leaves catch: coins of winter,
bronze butterflies. I see a gold windfall
of fantail gingkoes spin in the gutter.
If you were here you would tell me how all
the colors change with climate and with heat,
how you hauled wood from Leadville and Climax
from meadows above Red River near Midnite.
But now these leaves say only what I lack.
The mountain sends its gray message: fallow,
a scar of earth for snow to overgrow.

BAGATELLES

1.

Late at night, in the conservatory.

2.

A box of trifles, opened one by one.

3.

An emerald wrapped in a leaf.

4.

Those milky, bluewhite stones
my mother brought from Mexico
forty years ago.

5.

Another Sunday evening in thin light.
No miracles.

6.

Under the veneer, the wood splits.
Under the skin, the veins bulge.
No one, no one is home.

7.

A glossary of unintelligible words.
The perfume of the vernacular.

8.

Latissimus dorsi.
The dolphin muscles of your back.

9.
Your body tuned to love's first pitch,
the sound that broke the touch
by which we knew the other's grief.

10.
Here is the wind for you —
another bundle of syllables.

11.
Everyone is taking notes for infinity.

THE ISLAND

for George Scialabba

It was time to leave the island of regret.
Although rum was cheap and the local beer
was good and the coffee came from the slopes
of the blue volcanos, you had stayed long
enough, wearing a groove in the road that led
from the interior to the shore. Every day,
you would walk past the striped fishing boats —
Rosana, Mariana, Thiara, Carmen, Camille —
named for women you would never have time
to love, until you came to a small shrine
where you left fruit and flowers
for local deities. But you were tired
of the windfalls of coconuts and mangos,
the fish caught the first time you cast.
When you watched a net of clouds
moving too quickly across the sky,
you tried to forget you were on an island,
but you grew dizzy with incapability.
The dark was a name not worth repeating.
So you left while you still had wings
and the privacy of music to save you.
Now, talking in bed for hours, you lie here
beside me like Maya giving birth: an infinite
chain of Buddhas in each other's eyes.

PALINODE

I'll take it all back —
all the metaphors for sleep and love,
the anthropomorphisms of trees and plants,
the lunacy of trying to describe full moons,
the urge to elegize,
all the acrostics, puns, and palindromes —
I'll take it all back
and become a cartographer,
inserting the secret flaws in maps,
if only I can find the words
for the tenacity of the whippoorwill
before dawn by the railroad tracks —
almost like static, or white noise,
between flickers of light like lantern slides —
this nightjar jarring the night awake
for the nighthawks we imagine
ourselves to be.

III

―――――

Whoever you are: some evening take a step
out of your house, which you know so well.
Enormous space is near....

— Rainier Maria Rilke

THE ANNIVERSARIES

I.

You wake, your breath charged with dreams.
You are lightless years away. You need
one feather from an angel's wing, suspended
in a paperweight snowstorm, or
an Ojibway dream net, like a woven spiderweb,
to sort out the good dreams from the bad.
You dreamt of water, a smaller and smaller arc,
a whirlpool in which you were bathed
by an ancient woman. You dreamt you got stuck
in your mother's heavy satin wedding dress.
To get out, you had to rip some stitches,
a tiny cut, an episiotomy.

II.

The world laps on, a mad summary of calendar
squares. Each year, the date, a small scar,
reminds you. Leaves rain down, letters
on her grave. The tough sumac hangs on upstate.
This is the season of chrysanthemums,
the feast of the funeral flowers.
A man with a metal detector moves
through the gravestones. In the summer,
birds covered the columbarium.
You cleaned lime off her name.
But, November, birds gone, you hear
only the small gnawing sounds of earth.

SOLSTICE

The thin airmail paper bordered with bright, twining
flowers and covered with words in a not-quite-
familiar hand fell from a letter from my aunt.
Before I knew what it was, I started to read:

Dear Folks, In the nine weeks we have been here
we have been to one picture show. But tomorrow we are
going to go to a beautiful place called Horse-tail Falls.
Later, I'll send you the pictures we're going to take.

I received the Soc. Sections Mom sent. It looks like
I'll be the only single girl when I get home....
I've about decided I'm doomed to be an Old Maid.
But then I always did want to be a ministering angel.

I'd like a new point or two for my pen.
The old one has just about given out.
It is #3556. Osmeridium tip. Please ask Daddy
to see what he can do. Love, Beverly

It was 1947. She was twenty-one, in Mexico,
on a mission. After she came back to Salt Lake City,
she would marry another returned missionary,
have five children, and live for twenty-eight more years.

AT A CERTAIN DISTANCE

Today, on the highway,
I saw two coffin trucks, a sign
for Tommy's Sub Shop & Redemption Store,

and an invitation
to join the Espousal Center
of the Stigmatine Brothers.

Last night, as I searched
for long-playing records
in a department store,

my mother appeared to me
among the sewing machines
and notions of her former life.

In a mandorla of almond light
and a nimbus of tiny beads,
she asked, "Why are you surprised?

I'm always here, prodigal daughter."
And then, "Why do you live
in a house without mirrors?"

Why don't you have children? I hear,
though it seems to me my childhood
has nothing in it to mythologize,

the past become the present,
a roll of fogged film
miraculously transparent.

GRAVIDA

Grief fills the room up of my absent child,
Lies in his bed, walks up and down with me.
— Shakespeare, *King John*

Grief fills the room up,
leaves a blackened wreath
of locust and thorn.
I wanted to fill the house
with umbels of Queen Anne's lace.
Corbel and lintel, shutter and fanlight,
this house was yours.

I wanted to fill the house
with milk. Now a dry wind
sweeps the porch,
Cassiopeia rocks in the sky,
lullabies break and stutter
on the phonograph:
now I lay me now I lay now I now.

This is the borning room.
There should be herbs and pomanders.
There should be chests stained
with brick dust and sour milk,
with blueberries and buttermilk.
There should be lace curtains
and pieces of sea glass.

There should be you.
Not this scar, this cicatrix
marring my belly.
Not this rocking myself
to sleep each night
in a hush of words.

LETTER TO HUGO
FROM SEATTLE

Your voice that took us
down each cracked and salmon-
bucking creek is gone.
The firs are down.

In Pike Place Market
spice tea still sets
the air on fire with cloves
that mix with fish and brine.

And Skid Row drunks still pitch
to ferry docks and soup.
I danced here once, a new year
under neon cocktail signs.

My home is gone. My mother's
grave is all that's left,
like your White Center.
I'm seaward to the northeast now.

I see your face set totem-wise
near all that's left of towns
that scarcely had a name
before you wrote the name.

THE HOME COUNTIES
POSING AS THE
UNIVERSE

These are places I haven't seen
for twenty-five years. Even the chains
and brand names — Skaggs, Alpha Beta,
Arctic Circle — take me back
to childhood, though now I see
those two mysterious places
whose names I always loved — Sugarhouse
and Cottonwood — are only suburbs.

We drive past herds of black-faced sheep,
sage, and box elder trees —
I used to think box elders held
the ghosts of the Elders of the church.
On Mt. Timpanogas, a fall
of gold aspens still dazzles.
Put on thy beautiful garments,
O daughter of Zion.

When we get to Heber (that peculiar,
Mormon name), you tell me my mother
almost died here in the hot springs
when you were children.
Ten years after her death,
the family stories are surfacing —
black, scarred initials
on the aspens in the grove.

This is the place.
We will make the desert bloom.
— Canyons of condos, valleys of golf courses.
But there is still one small cemetery,
a river full of gravestones
and the last flowers before frost,
that winds between highway and bluff,
answering to our names.

DESERT LANDS OF UTAH

Growing blind, my stepgrandmother says,
"Growing old is heck."
Gran can't see Grandpa's slideshows anymore.
Shades drawn in the late afternoon,
we're watching "Desert Lands of Utah"
(First Prize from the Photochrome Club),
instead of the family slides I asked to see.
"This one I call 'Herding the Sheep,'
and this one is 'On the Rim,' " he says.
Such human, inadequate names.
I see the motes in the projector's beam
fall across Gran's unblinking eyes.

She wants him to put on the music
that goes with the slides.
"Temple at Sinawava" scorches around the edges
as he looks for the tape.
"Never mind the music; it doesn't matter anymore,"
she calls out to him.
"I was just doing what you asked, Virginia."
Back to the slides, he only strays once
from his set narrative to say something about
the trip they took where he captured these shots.
"That was Verda," she says, "not me;
you went on that trip with Verda thirty years ago."

"At Delicate Arch," he resumes, pointing
at the slide, "that man I used for scale
disappeared after I clicked the shutter.
He had a heart attack, fell

backward into the gorge.
They had to haul his body out with mules."
He's told that story so many times
he almost thinks it's funny.
In his photographs, the people
are included mostly for scale.
That's why there are hardly any pictures
of my grandma, my mother, the grandchildren.

After the last slide, "Moab at Sunset,"
I tell my grandfather I want a photograph
to remember my visit by. He's reluctant,
but we go outside. Evening light reflects
off the Wasatch Range and bounces
over to the strip mine ridges
across Salt Lake Valley. He sets up
a tripod and timer, then stands beside me.
I put my arm across his back. At eighty,
he's still as taut and straight
as the Colorado River at Dead Horse Point.
This is as close as we will get.

PATRILINEAGE

I.
February. Hunger moon. Cold,
dense air, the beach weighted

with breast-shaped stones and
crescents of bottle glass.

As I watch the tide lift the ice
floes off the marsh grass,

the unresolved images converge
in my grandfather's binoculars.

"Where are my tools?" he asks.
"I'm lost without my tools."

He lives in a chaos of broken
clocks and rulers.

I have inherited his looped
fingerprints and possibly

the confused whorls of his brain,
a lattice of lucidity and fog.

II.
My father sits in the dark
scripture of his life.

He cannot hear me calling him
through the plain tenor of his grief.

All day I watch the field change —
everything changes except the black

rectangular opening into the barn loft.
No light ever goes there.

At night, my father put his glass eye
on a shelf in the medicine chest.

God's omniscience was in my father's eye.
When I reached for my toothbrush,

I could see the little painted-on
capillaries and the blue

filaments in the iris.
The hard light it emanated.

COEUR D'ALENE

For years he secreted shards of words,
a magpie of language. Words creased
the corners of his mouth like letters

folded and unfolded too many times.
Now, his own face is a stranger's.
He looks at himself in the mirror and says:

"He bothers me; I want him out of my room."
It's as baffling as the Hitchcock story
where the murder weapon, a frozen

leg of lamb, is cooking in the oven
by the time the detective arrives.
As if the icicle driven through the brain

has melted: no weapon, no fingerprints.
Who he was has vanished into the snow.
It's been a long time since

the unglazed light of day touched him.
All our names are lost
in his artificial wakefulness.

I wait in a nerveless way for sleep
or something better to take him farther
than we can follow, where shadows

of birds sweep over his childhood body:
body of light, body of time,
full of joy in the humming field.

QUARRY

Nineteen, lonely, making pies in the Abigail Tea Room,
you ride your bike through a landscape pitted and gouged,
reddish and lunar. The season of catalpas —

fragile white cups, maroon veins, bright pollen spots —
is past. You ride until you come to the quarry,
water covering the scars, trilobites, facets

of your fossil self. You swim, the water brims,
but does not spill, coats you with limestone dust —
chalky, mild, a blessing. When you return

to your room above the restaurant, full of beds
and buffalo flies, someone has left on your doorstep
a coffee cup full of asters, honeysuckle, buttercups.

And Venus is rising over the meadow, the light
lavender as if filtered through old glass.

MY SISTER SWIMMING
SIDE BY SIDE

Gently balancing on the wing
of an intelligent whirlwind,
in parallel desire,
my sister, swimming side by side.

— Charles Baudelaire

We swim out of darkness and into light,
the water a swarm of bees on our skin.
The world blurs a little around the edges,
but I feel you close beside, matching me
stroke for stroke the length of the pool.

Like two dolphins turning, we turn,
smooth and synchronized, unplanned radar.
For nearly a mile, we swim like this,
before something breaks my stroke —
a thought of my above-water life,
so different from this world
where everything is simplified and sleek.

Days later we speak about how we swam
together, how even if we planned it,
we could not do it again: our parallel desire
rising and surfacing like the water
that bound us long before this.

HOW TO NAVIGATE
SMALL BODIES OF WATER

You could be a dragonfly, leaving your
nymph behind, drying your lace-veined
wings on a leaf. You want fear,
you want light, you want too much.
Under the ice, the elegies go on.
Body by body, we are swimming
in our separate channels, swimming
out our losses, the way we read
long novels. This is a pond
like a ruin, a perfect contusion.
Neutral. Blue afternoon.
Paper boats. Birthday suits.
It's a strange soup you live in,
little fish. You stem a slim tide.

DREAM

From that far country,
my mother has sent me
instead of a telegram
a mammogram.

In the cloudy light,
I can see our two fates
in its map.
I can see the continental

drift of the two islands,
the amniotic lakes.
Breasts,
the radiologist tells me,

are symmetrical
like butterfly wings.
If the symmetry fails,
the body will fall ill.

SISTER DUST

The x-ray shows a mass, a blur,
the body

you thought you had
not there.

Until you wake in the hospital,
you won't know.

Travel the sick heart
inland

to the coarse flesh
of desire,

born to salt and thirst,
to the west —

home   space   light —
dizzy with it,

as if this were an ordinary
forgetting,

an orchard flowering where
knowledge ends.

W I N D F A L L

The limbo of the city
yields to the last apples,
a scrawl of ivy,

a peculiar tint of sky
— russet, russet —
above the orchard.

We sit on a stump
breaking the symmetry
of the rows of trees.

Woodsmoke and fear
camouflage three deer.
Scarcely enough time

to eat a peck of apples,
burn a cord of wood,
find what's elemental.

Some apples
— heavy in their skins —
look nearly perfect

until we touch them,
find them soft and spoiled.
One apple,

polished like a mirage,
is diminished
to a perfection

we can't achieve.
What goes on beneath
quickens.

HOW TO USE
A COMA KIT

Sleeper, you are me, stripped down to bed,
bedclothes. Out of this black bag,
black weather, I bring not the usual pins
and feathers, but this kit of sensations —
smell of mown hay, raspberries,
honeysuckle, cow dung and burning rubber;
sound of church bells and train whistles,
screeching cats and crying babies —
to stimulate P 300, the specific wave form
that indicates surprise, or symptoms
of memory. The birches outside your window
change colors fifty times a day.
Do you know that? What lament can reach you?
Sleeper, your beauty is fleeing, fleeting.

E L E G Y

in memory of Trudy Villars (1947-1990)

It's May. In the blue-and-white bandbox
of St. Mary's, we all look terribly old.
This time, the bruises under our eyes
won't be undone.

Grief lavish as the blossomed light
and hard as these pews, I can't kneel.
I can't murmur prayers with the priest.
I can't sing.

You got smaller and smaller. Your bones
light as kitesticks, your body a paper
lantern with only your heart to flush
and fill it.

Kai says you have gone into a fish.
A rainbow fish seen through a glass boat.
Free to move among the coral.
Free to move.

As we drive home, the light lasts
a long time, the sky never quite
darkening. The earth doesn't want
to let you go.

FORESHADOW

As if you had gone around a corner
and were coming back, I will find
your footprints in the snow
for days after you leave.

It is beautiful here. It will still
be beautiful. In the January dusk,
long, feathered shadows fall
from the pines along the road.

Rabbits' feet and fox paws engrave
your path with blue-gray patterns.
Other tracks will inscribe layers
on layers of hieroglyphs I cannot read.

A single contrail will arrow the sky.
The wind will blow the snow to dust:
here we spoke of . . . here . . . and here.
I will fill my notebooks with sleep.

WATERLILIES IN
THE MUDDY RIVER

Waking to riverlight and pulse of traffic
on Storrow Drive, you go to the window
and see that, almost overnight, green discs
of waterlilies have spilled into this inlet

of the Muddy River, part of Olmsted's
nearly vanished Emerald Necklace.
These are not Monet's *Nymphéas*,
rising and dissolving into air:

these are heavy, rooted in the dark river.
Underneath, swimming among strong stems,
you know there are carp, orange and lucent.
You know rivers and the names for pain,

and when you touch me, my body
becomes transparent. You know
what the rhythms of my blood mean.
And as I watch your eyes skim the river,

I want you to know — whatever this room holds,
whatever I hold for you — these lilies survive,
and chicory and crickets fill the fields
of late summer, even in the city.

SUE STANDING's previous poetry books are *Amphibious Weather* and *Deception Pass*. Director of the Creative Writing Program at Wheaton College, she teaches creative writing and African literature. Among the grants she has received are a Bunting Institute Fellowship, a National Endowment for the Arts fellowship, a Fulbright-Hays Summer Seminar Grant to study Indian literature in India, and a Whiting Foundation Travel Grant to do research on African literature in West Africa. She lives in Cambridge, Massachusetts.